# Nothing Is So Lovely

*poems by*

# Candace Butler

*Finishing Line Press*
Georgetown, Kentucky

# Nothing Is So Lovely

## ACKNOWLEDGMENTS

I thank God first and foremost. I thank the numerous amazing writers, mentors,
colleagues, and friends who've helped and supported me. I'm grateful for the
superb creative writing program at Antioch University of Los Angeles. I thank
my incredible family for their love and support.

Acknowledgment is made to the editors of the following publications in which
some of these poems—sometimes in different versions—first appeared: "Dear
Seymour," *One*, Issue 4; "Elephants," *RiverLit*'s 100 Word Challenge; "In the City,"
*Clamor*, 2014 Issue; "Still Life," *The Pikeville Review*, Spring 2015 Issue; "The
Crooked Road," *Dirty Chai*, Issue Two: *Adventureland* and *Silver Birch Press*'
Where I Live Poetry & Photography Series; and "White Wire," *Prime Number
Magazine*, Prime Decimals Issue 67.2.

Cover image is Martin Schongauer's *The Archangel Gabriel* c. 1490-1 from the
Rosenwald Collection at the National Gallery of Art in Washington, D.C.

Publisher: Leah Maines

Editor: Christen Kincaid

Cover Art: Martin Schongauer, Courtesy National Gallery of Art, Washington

Author Photo: Freda Butler

Cover Design: Candace Butler

Printed in the USA on acid-free paper.
Order online: www.finishinglinepress.com
also available on amazon.com

Author inquiries and mail orders:
Finishing Line Press
P. O. Box 1626
Georgetown, Kentucky 40324
U. S. A.

# Table of Contents

*for Isabel*

*and all storytellers passing down life's stories*

## Appalachian Turkey

The turkey by the elderberry
has seen a hundred of me.
Her cane legs warp beneath
that sagging mass and hanging neck
until I half expect words to drip from that beak
word, word, word;
a faucet telling the same story
to different people.

He whittled you a little basket out of a peach pit?
I know, but tell me
while you pick at your path
and gnaw at your grave,
while I sit, vein to pencil,
counting my children before they're born.

## At the Farmer's Market

On a humid, late summer morning,
framed beneath great iron arches,
empty train tracks waiting in the background
for the next long rattling chain of cars,
by the stack of fuzzy peaches,
being pushed in a wheelchair by,
presumably, her daughter,
is a woman with gray hair
and a string of tired pearls resting on
her lacy collar, her linen dress,
covering up her blue veins at the wrist.
She is telling a story about peaches, how
she and her brothers and sister
as children in Georgia
would be taken to the peach fields
to pick all they could eat. Her
eyes glint like rare gems beneath
her arching eyebrows, her knuckles
clutch tighter to her purse, she
tells how they bit into the great orbs,
the juice running down their chins.
On their nice Sunday clothes,
the juice of all those peaches.
And now her daughter, I guess it is,
wheels her into the bright and spectacular sunlight,
the last bit of story still dripping from her chin.

**Bear Ridge**
*where I was born and raised*


All I know of the world is milkweed fuzz
blowing past the sinewy
call of the coyote, the red glimpse of a fox,
decorous glint of dew,
evergreen bowing to the sky, that roy g biv
fleeting past the grounded mushroom, a stalk with bright tutu.
Gentle wings of the hummingbird beat,
handbell birds chime from distant trees.
I know the beauty that the moon must overhear:
jagged leaves of elms rustling colloq,
knuckley apple trees swaying, beehive buzzing in a treetop,
lady's slipper sleeping to the cricket's song full of vibrato,
minute whooshing of the wind from mountain to mountain.
Nothing is so lovely as the blooming of wild plum
or the rising up of underground springs and the heirloom daffodil,
pawpaw's mango-banana custard fruit, the seedy field to pack
queen anne's lace to the brim. Radio playing local musicians by a dj,
rabbits running across dusty roads through red clover, and I
see more splendor following a deer path
through a grove of sugar maples, past cool creeks, circling
unkempt thickets, walking over the trail of cloven hoof.
Valleys hold the sounds that echo from the mountain, a golden eagle
wakes in a high branch to the small worms that drilled
xylographs in tree bark, the graceful and archaic
yonahlossee salamander walks on the moss-covered, rocky knob,
zillions of mold spores settle everywhere. This is Appalachia.

## Beyond the Surface

I am a painting on the wall.
The wall is spackled behind me,
but I don't mind.

They can't get me out of the portrait.
They scratch on my eyes and
my crimson and lemon skin,

They try to rub off my smile
and claw at my clothes,
but I won't come off the wall.

They call in another artist
to paint another scene
on top of me, to cover me up.

As the paint dries above me,
they are happy with this;
they leave me as I am.

In the night, the paint buckles,
peels, falls to the floor in ribbons
below me.

Again I stare out at the world.

**Calla Lillies**
*after Diego Rivera's El Vendedor de Alcatraces*


My shin bones
called for nimbuses,
an empty ache
like longing.

My hand
to your chest
sinks and swells,
silver-haired moss
drunken
on rainfall.

I pluck
the shapely white flowers
that grow there,
bring them
inside,
and let them
die there on
the kitchen counter
beside a vase
full of water.

We always knew
we'd outlive them;
are their white carcasses
still beautiful?

## Dear Seymour

*after Dalí's "The Fallen Angel,"*
*an illustration for Dante's "Divine Comedy"*

There's an angel with papery skin
disrobed of his soft nimbus raiment.
That's a common dream, I believe, nudity.
His holey wings are a sickly green.

Disrobed of his soft nimbus raiment,
the angel pulls open the drawer to his heart;
his holey wings are a sickly green.
His bones push through the skin.

The angel pulls open the drawer to his heart;
fingers claw at the drawer to his gut.
His bones push through the skin.
There's nothing but emptiness inside.

Fingers claw at the drawer of a groin.
You never find what you're looking for;
there's nothing but emptiness inside.
Toes twisted, sinking through clouds,

you never find what you're looking for.
My guardian angel has nightmares of falling:
toes twisted, sinking through clouds.
*It's not the same*, he whispers, *it's not the same.*

My guardian angel has nightmares of falling.
That's a common dream, I believe.
*It's not the same, no, it's not the same,*
whispers the angel with papery skin.

## Elephants
*after Dalí*


Here in the desert of your mind
is a black striped bass.
Heat waves rise from the vibrating
strings. The hand that plucks
is the hand that frees.
The teeth that bite
have a lifetime of need
to gnaw through the unreliable,
through matte ancestors
and sober eagles,
through the bubble blower's
mouthful, the natural liking,
the little hole for lace,
the lusterless finish,
the pushover, the obligation,
through the open window
and the forever wild
and into the fragrance
of one man's dream
about elephants with long, thin legs
he could pluck like strings.

## How to Make Angel Food

First you drop through wild grapevines
to pick up a guru right from her home
and walk through heavy fog on Bear Ridge
to bring along an old-timey song catcher,
then head on over to a luthier workshop
just over the mountain to get a respected picker
and his daughter crafting guitar number 684.

Follow the sound that's handed down from generations in a
family up the second-highest peak, where a fiddler unites with
a banjo player in song and dance, and sidestep just off the
crooked road to lure the writer away from the harvest table.
Follow along the cool, clear creeks and sugar maples where
you'll pull a poet away from her line and verse and into your
bowl. Sift and resift six times. Beat with wire whip.

Gradually blend in words. Mix in their stories, hopes,
and dreams in several portions, folding them in gently.
Bake in a moderately slow oven until they're golden
and spring back when lightly pressed with finger tip.
Invert pan over the neck of a mountain dew bottle.
Leave inverted until thoroughly cooled.
10 to 12 servings.

## In the City

Two children
are playing on the bus.
The mothers
are talking in Spanish.

Outside the windows,
the trees grow old and fat.
They lean into the street,
over the bus,
to listen.

## In the Classroom

He can't remember what day it was
or what he was doing,
maybe a Tuesday, maybe
watching *Pulp Fiction*,
maybe grading projects—he is,
after all, a professor—
when he looked over and
there she was, his girlfriend,
back curled the most
beautiful contour he
had ever seen, the bone
of her cheek pressed to
the bone of her knee,
her hair flowing just out
of her eye, a piece perfectly
out of place, but instead
of saying, *I love you*
he said, "don't move," and
he reached for the camera.
When he turned back
around, she had straightened
her back, moved her hair,
posed, and the light now hit her
grotesquely. He may have
shuddered along with the lens,
maybe said "never mind."

A student's voice from the corner
is encouraging him to continue.
He picks up his dry erase marker,
waves it in the air,
never mind.

## In Time

A newborn fawn curls up beside a yellow can in time.
It will grow and leap and run and learn to stand in time.

*Gold Lube: sealed for your protection* reads the can.
We will know the irony, we'll understand, in time.

Holes rusting right through, holes rusting right through.
Tall grass will grow around that rusty yellow can in time.

Immigrants will come to bale that grass now yellowed.
Oh what is carried in, and what off, this land in time.

They haul the bales in beds of trucks down the road again.
Seeds in the ground become fodder in the hand in time.

Even with a tarp atop the rows and rows of hay bales,
a few splinters pull apart, blow away, stranded in time.

Like faces in old yearbooks, the writer, the artist, the butler,
a few always fall along the way. Lost, abandoned, in time.

## Living on the Mountain

The pine is foaming at the mouth,
whiskers stand on end,
bark snaps fast and vicious
as the turkey jumps the fence.

A lone cow is mooing at night,
the stars are cloaked in clouds,
fireflies mimic stars above
drops of rain that never make it to the ground,
soaking into blades of grass,
reappearing in the morning a thick dew.

We sink to the shadows,
we shrink away.

Barbed wire, you tangled rusty mess,
how does it feel to be eaten by trees?—
to kill small animals who skid across you,
you as startled, as shaking for minutes, as they are?

The trumpets rise in silence from the earth,
from emptiness and sleep.
Air passes through them,
how lives are spent—air in, air out.
The lungs are monasteries hung on cliffs of rib,
devout.

The sloping giant's call wisps through the screen
fainter and fainter.

## On the Back of the Dragon

Let's watch the painted leaves dance 'round the mountain.
The four winds of the earth are such polite
partners, always leading, stepping lightly on the mountain.
It is their hardwood floor, the sacred mountain—
watch the way they tiptoe over her scars.
And watch, there is an angel on the mountain—
another one ascending from the east. The mountain
is full of hurt, full of pain, has closed its eyes,
refused to budge. The angel's eyes
protect the sea, something the mountain
can barely see, and all of us in silence,
all we know of life and love we know in silence.

All we know of music, too, is the silence
when it's gone. All we know of rest is work; the mountain,
our ruthless protector, waits to watch us live in silence;
even the angels fall upon their faces here in silence.
It is here that we are saved to be polite.
God shall wipe away our tears in silence.
And we shall thirst no more, sweat no more, in silence.
We walk across the mountain's scars,
knowing that these are our scars.
Oh the world we love and wreck, at once, in silence.
You haven't stared as long as me into the eyes
of a young buck, his quick stomp, his unending eyes.

Let's find the music; let's open our eyes.
For the space of half an hour, there is silence.
A huge big room filled with nothing but eyes.
The men with old and watery eyes, the children's eyes
wide as the base of the mountain,
the young woman with hair that hides her eyes,
the ten year old boy who asks an adult to dance, his eyes
watching everyone else, his elbows—everyone's elbows—polite.
The band is in the corner, with their polite
and searching eyes.
Their fingertips like lightning, fingertips with scars.
We hold our hands out in the light and never see the scars.

There is a kind of incense, smoke that rises and it scars;
you notice it like a holy woman in prayer, a fire in the eyes.
Voices, thunderings, lightnings, memory that scars.
The dust in lungs of their fast feet, internal scars.
The seven pickers poised to sound and trapped in silence.
The first sounds, feet of hail and fire leave the earth with scars;
the trees burn up, we cannot breathe, the open grass, all scars.
The second sounds; it's as if the whole great mountain
has caught fire and fallen in the sea. Oh, but the mountain
is still standing, and so are we. Now third is the fiddle, pulling the stars
down around our heads, burning like a lamp. So many men, polite
as can be, die to the sidelines; they are polite.

And the singer now sounds a voice that makes the polite
moon darken, the sun becomes smitten; I feel the scars
on his fingers as we twirl up the line again. The polite
nod of my next partner; woe, woe, woe, a polite
voice calls; apparently there is always more to come. Our eyes
burn like fallen stars turning into keys. No matter how polite
we are, no matter how polite,
we want them on their knees. We want to feel a recklessness that silence
can't take back. We turn and turn, one last time, and this man, so polite,
these days we seek to dance 'til death and cannot find it on the mountain.
We still dance fire, leave our scars, upon the mountain.

The last note has yet to sound upon the mountain;
our fingertips hold the power to set it on fire. Our polite
handshakes always covered with these scars.
The painted leaves are forever seared like golden flecks into our eyes
that we hand down, hand down, hand down to our children in silence.

## Song of the Mountains

The night, the constellations,
push in on our roofs.
We cannot tell if the pops and creaks
are our cooling houses
or aging joints.
We have spurts of inactivity,
where we stiffen
and some of us break.

Morning comes,
the messenger bee hums its welcome.
We, too, hum while we work.
Our skin is like layers of sediment,
fields of grace,
gardens.
What do we sow?
What do we weep?
Tears like rice fields in the east.

What is poured in us
like measuring cups?
Poured back out
from our pursed lips,
poured into the air,
into our ears.

The mountain calls it moments;
the musician calls it years.

## Still Life
*after Ruysch*


I want the silk of blueberries
without the softening centers;
I want all the shades of dusk in one small fruit.

I want the cobalt salamander
uncovered from the shadows,
I want to see the small steel specks along its back.

I want the leafy vine of cantaloupe
haloing the citron melon;
I want the maze of rind, the subtle green.

I want the cerulean fringe of chicory
floating in the air, highlighted hue;
I want a ray of light through this dark space.

I want the chubby blush of peaches
laying leisurely in stacks;
I want them forever framed by fine-toothed leaves.

I want the partitioned pomegranate
always sliced at its alzarin prime;
I want the rosy seeds, the film of white.

And I want the horsehair nest
before the fragile, soft eggs hatch;
I want the fear of breaking at every touch.

## Ten Minute Nude
*from a life drawing class and 1 Corinthians 6:19*


Your body is a sanctuary.
Marble skin: cold but smooth.
Early morning sunlight
shines through the window.
Still model; her breath is shallow,
                    time waits.


Quick, charcoal-covered fingers
smudge in soft shadows.


Your body is a sanctuary.
The façade hidden in shadows;
the stained heart full of light.
And that light shifts,
the frame shifts,
             time
                  shifts.


A halo of light wraps around
shiny hair that veils the face.


Your body is a sanctuary.
Elbow akimbo, thin arm crossing the backbone,
lines of ribs like pews
below a gentle, congregating light.
A few precise strokes shroud newsprint;
a trace of you is all that's left.

## The Cornstalk's Dance

I watch your cornsilk hair
rotting in the sun,
your stalky neck swaying
in the breeze—you lunatic,
dancing with me in the daylight
like its moonlight, never caring
that your spine is bending double,
always double,
stringy fingers like to mumble
in the wind,
bend, bend, lower, lower
lay your spiked crown on the ground.
Rustle—but don't rouse from slumber.
Now it's time to brown.

## The Crooked Road

The next time you drive through
the mountains of southern Virginia,
take a couple of long, winding roads
out of your way. Stop at a small gas
station with bags on the pump handles.
Fold up your map
with its road numbers and compass
and ask the person leaning
on an elbow at the counter
how to get back to the interstate,
you've made a wrong turn.
Listen to the directions:
right past the silo,
take a left when you see the three
big crosses (you can't miss them),
then there will be a fork in the road,
and you'll want to stay toward the left.
From there you go about, oh I don't know,
what would you say, a few miles?
A few miles. And you should be able to
find the interstate and follow the signs
from there. Before you go, browse the
couple of aisles, pass by the baby food jars
with expiration dates nearly eight years past,
the rows of gum and candy bars in dust.
Settle for an overpriced drink or
a lottery ticket.
Look closely at the peeling sticker
on the slush puppy machine by the register;
it will be cracked teal where
there used to be a deep ultramarine.
The corners will be peeling, a sticky
border where they used to lay flat.
Once you pay, follow the directions.

Chant them over the low murmur
of the radio. Listen close, now,
this is the most important part:
look at every wild grapevine,
feel the depth of the forest, take in
the "Jesus loves you" graffiti
on a gutted trailer in an overgrown field.

You might never find this place again.

## The Hanging

Clasped high among the mountains in the morning,
the bedsheet flaps on the clothesline as she pins it up to dry.
Her red nails dance at the ends of age-spotted fingers.
Her heels grind down into the stool she uses to reach up high;
her eyes look on as she folds the corners—never looking,
the way the merchant must hang bright, silken sheets to billow
in some marketplace halfway across the earth.

I lean against the locust tree and watch and offer nothing.

## The Mountain

I.

The sky is a flat, metal roll
in an upright player piano,
turning, turning, though the song's been ruined.
Sometimes that paper catches, and tears,
and for a second you can glimpse the other side—
that other world that shines dimly on
the bales of hay in solemn rows
setting 'longside the wooden fence like hammers-in-waiting.
See the holes, child? See the wrinkles.
See Pluto in the sharp night air, off to the right,
a wearhole slightly larger than the rest in that ersatz sky.
Cattle dance on queen anne's lace.

There booms a slow legato;
even bullets shed their shells to fly.

II.

Children play out in the abandoned open.
Their golden pigs and saccharin bulls
are nothing compared to the porcelain cow
in my mother's cabinet—
I bought it myself in a country I've never seen.
The edges of the forest now are fluted,
the front door hasn't matched its frame for years.
Iodine hangnails scream against the gutter,
grin and whisper, "squirrel away your shackles,"
my shrine to disremembrance
will fold itself when put away
in its lexical bed of flames.

No one shakes with fear of your words like I do;
No one shakes like me.

III.

By a farm of mud, a field of grace,
the mountain bows its head before the mill,
baring endless rows of spruce sapling plugs
atop that scraggly skull:
four hundred needled masts foundering
in a choppy scalp of dirt.
The evergreen rhododendron knows
silence is a wary acclamation.
The dumb, deaf worms still etch John's seminary;
they bore us pity in a windblown pine.
You don't know this land like I do—
the trees are left to grow too tall for use.

The veins of coal only run so deep;
we've known that all along.

IV.

A donkey gallops across a hill
beneath a cold and hazy sky
that overturns our wicker chairs,
past a chimney standing alone in an empty field,
crumbling at the bottom
like a stick of butter melting in the pan.

The wind got up last night,
the forest of springs beneath creaking gently
under the lifted weight.
Now the draft is here to stay,
the bed we made unmaking—
for you are here to weight it down no more,
and all I know of hell is that you get to choose your torture;
all I know of hell is that we are already there.

## White Wire

Fence my eyes with chicken wire;
call me your foiled bride.
the pale pink darnings of yestercade are nothing more
than a forgotten study on a dusty floor.
the white lace train hocks over
the mountain, hunching its back against the cold.
the woodstove of my childhood will
asphyxiate me yet.

The only color I'll know now is dried flowers
tied with ribbon in a closet in a shoebox in the snow.
My reed neck in biplicity,
my domed cathedral of a throat
lying dormant like hornets in a nest of spit—
who tells them to hum the score you wrote for me?

## Who

I

Who pinned the streamers on your handlebar mustache?
You who told me saffron was an herb before a color,
your chrome teeth glinting fast through parted lips.
and soon your leather hands wax old,
my golden insides turning at your touch.
I've known only of round-trip journeys:
labyrinths of trees and gravel
on roads lined by crosses.

In what corners I cower to stay pale,
branded by choice
and armed with a lust for *Köhlerglaubes*.
My motheaten bones long for the land.
They push against my skin that barks in pain,
and hunker down in droves against my feet.

And the petals fall like rain,
and the petals fall like rain.

II

Your air is of ginseng stock—
and no one drinks as much as me
or strangles near as often.
In our shadowboxing days,
full of flowers flattened in wax paper,
I wrote you letter after letter,
dozens of words herded about
the page by a weary hand.

I've gathered rocks with a child,
and walked in the footprints of horses.
Now there is a fingerprint on the mirror
I like to never saw for looking.
No wonder you forgot it
when you packed up and left.

III

The crinoline bushes rustle,
their soft, bruised hands always watching
from their window over skillets of water and air.
The mourning dove calls me back in
at night from the shadows
with that truth-shucked tongue
that lingers smooth and calm
on thyme breath, "who?"
With that tender voice
that grinds my bones to ashes
and drives my tears from their skullward homes,
I'll get a hold of your exhausted memory yet.
Oh, you partaker of thread and needles,

do not call for me when I am banqueting on grief.

Candace Butler is an American poet and writer. She resides in her hometown of Sugar Grove, Virginia located in the South Central region of the Appalachian Mountains with the Jefferson National Forest as her backyard. She holds a Master of Fine Arts in Creative Writing with a mixed concentration in poetry and creative nonfiction from Antioch University of Los Angeles. She holds a Bachelor of Arts in English Literature & Creative Writing, a Bachelor of Fine Arts in Art with a Graphic Design concentration, and a Minor in Mathematics. Butler is an Adjunct Professor of English at Emory & Henry College. She is a 'Round the Mountain artisan in Southwest Virginia's Artisan Network and Entertainment Chairperson for the annual Hungry Mother Festival held in Hungry Mother State Park, Marion, Virginia. She is former co-poetry editor of online literary magazine *Lunch Ticket*. Butler's first chapbook of poetry is *Royal Crown* (2014). Butler's poetry also appears or is forthcoming in numerous print and online journals and anthologies, including *Anthology of Appalachian Writers: Nikki Giovanni Volume VIII, One, Prime Number Magazine, The Pikeville Review, Clamor, RiverLit, Pure Coincidence, About Place Journal, Eclectica Magazine, 3 Elements Review, Silver Birch Press, Kind of a Hurricane Press,* and others. A comprehensive list of Butler's publications is at www.candacebutler.com.